Keep The Wall

(A study for born again church members …

and the responsibility that comes with being part of
God's family in a local church.)

By: J. Llewellyn

Introduction

I'm thankful for the opportunity to share with you my love for the body of Christ that we affectionately refer to as The Church. Raised in a godly home, I've never known a time in which I was not part of a local assembly of believers. Would to God that I could say I have always acted according to God's word, but sadly I have fallen short many times. I felt compelled to write what the Lord has helped me to understand throughout my life as a born-again believer and church member. Being part of a local assembly comes with serious responsibilities, whether it be as a part of the congregation or leadership. We have a job to do. The lost must be reached before it's too late, and we have an adversary who would love nothing more than to tangle God's people in a web of strife, contention, and confusion as souls fall into eternity without God. I pray this study will encourage the true saints to strive for unity as we press toward the mark for the prize of the high calling of God. May we be found faithful as the day of His appearing approaches.

Keep The Wall

(A study for born again church members ...

and the responsibility that comes with being a part of God's family in the local church.)

In the Book of Nehemiah, we find God's people working to repair the walls of Jerusalem. They had a mind to work, and Nehemiah was determined to bring honor to the Lord God of Israel. However, when the people began working together with one mind and one purpose, the enemy came up against them. Nehemiah was compelled to set watches on the wall to protect the work.

That said, I believe one of the greatest dangers of any church is to fall to an enemy they have never recognized or acknowledged as formidable. The walls are left unattended while the enemy scales over and gets inside. We are told plainly in I Peter 5:8 that we have an adversary who "walketh about, seeking whom he may devour." We are also instructed in Ephesians 6:11 to "put on the whole armour of God, that ye may be able to stand against the wiles of the devil." I'm convinced that too many soldiers are going to battle having never been prepared. A soldier who has no idea how to identify the enemy or never briefed on his tactics and devices, would be an easy target ... and sure to fall in the line of duty.

So, how do we identify our adversary and arm ourselves with knowledge concerning his tactics? I believe God's Word tells us all we need to know of his characteristics and methods. I've come to understand how methodical our opponent really is. He never moves without a complete blueprint of how to kill, steal, and ultimately destroy.

Each one who has placed their trust in Christ has a responsibility to honor and respect God's laws. Biblical laws and commandments are in place to help us stay close to Him as we travel through this life. It's also important to understand that when we are accepted into a fellowship of believers to worship together, we are responsible to that body of believers, as well. Individuals who conduct themselves in a sinful and wreckless manner in the community will also bring reproach on the church fellowship with which they are associated. Likewise, we must know how to conduct ourselves inside the church.

Satan's plan is to buffet the church and we MUST be aware how he plans to do it if we are to emerge a victorious congregation of believers with an effective testimony for Christ in our respective communities. This study is by no means a glorification of our adversary, but rather a flag of awareness to his tactics, and how we can use an understanding of God's word to overcome the snares in our path. First, it's important to understand his physical traits. Satan is referred to as the serpent.

I – Adversary Identification

The Common Characteristics Of A Serpent:

Forked tongue

In Psalms 140:1-3, David beseeches God to deliver him from the evil men who, "have sharpened their tongues like a serpent; adder's poison is under their lips."

Carnivore lifestyle

All known snakes (with only one exception) seek to eat the living with the goal of completely devouring, leaving nothing behind. Satan desires to devour you! (I Peter 5:8)

Extremely flexible

I Corinthians 11:14,15 "for Satan himself is transformed into an angel of light, Therefore, it is no great thing if his ministers (helpers) also be transformed as the ministers of righteousness." Someone or something may seem completely harmless - even religious, but very, very dangerous.

Death by a quick bite or a slow, gradual constriction

Satan can bring an unexpected crisis, but his best method is a slow and gradual squeeze. The 'squeeze' is effective because it is so gradual, the prey doesn't begin to suffer until the squeeze has become so tight, there is no way of escape – unless the snake itself is killed. That's where Christ comes in. When we call on His name, he will 'loosen' us from the contraction of sin.

Beguiling

Satan is beguiling which is the direct opposite of Christ who 1 Peter 2:22 states, "… committed no sin, neither was any guile found in his mouth."

The definition of beguile is as follows: To mislead by craft or artifice. (Artifice – To invent lies.)

Capable of blending in to its environment

I John 4:1 "Beloved, believe not every spirit, but try the spirits whether they are of God."

John 7:24 "Judge not according to the appearance, but judge righteous judgment."

A false individual or device can blend in to a body of believers quite easily and work behind the scenes, causing division.

II – The Adversary's Methods

Step 1: The Doubting of God's Word or the Integrity of Another True Believer

A question in and of itself is not wrong, depending on the motive of the heart. A loving brother or sister in Christ may be confused on a matter and need clarification. This comes from a pure heart genuinely seeking truth. This question is also handled discretely and respectfully. However, there are two other types of questions meant to destroy fellowship. I believe we can find these three types of questions in the scriptures and New Testament epistles to expose the motive.

Type One Question: Of a pure heart for the purpose of seeking the truth.

Example: Acts 16:30 The keeper of prison asked of Paul and Silas, "Sirs, what must I do to be saved?"

Example: John 3 Nicodemus to Jesus "How can a man be born when he is old?"

James 3:17 tells us that "wisdom from above is first pure, then peaceable, gentle, and **easy to be intreated.**"

A loving, and spiritually-discerning church leader will understand when someone is genuinely seeking answers, but he will also guard the ministry against 'foolish questions' as instructed in Titus 3:9. "For they are unprofitable and vain." Unprofitable, meaning someone who isn't asking a question to profit knowledge or a better understanding, and "vain", meaning an individual who is asking a question for the sole purpose of making someone appear inadequate while puffing up his own ego. This will be covered under the Type Three Question.

Type Two Question: Satan's Device used for the purpose of bringing doubt concerning the integrity of another true brother or sister.

Genesis 3:1 Satan to Eve "Yea, hath God said, Ye shall not eat of every tree of the garden?"

Satan had to paint an image of himself to Eve. He had to make her believe that God was out to inhibit her, while HE wanted to help enlighten her. (Satan's lie) - If she would listen to him, she would be enlightened to a more successful and free life.

Examples: Do you think that was the right thing to do? What do you think about that situation? Don't you think that should've been handled differently? I know God's word says this, but don't you think it should be interpreted to fit our culture?

For the more personal issues that may arise, each member of a congregation must understand that a certain amount of trust is necessary on the part of a congregation in regard to the Pastor and Elders who are sometimes privy to information they are not at liberty to disclose to the entire congregation. In spite of the Information Age in which we live, NO ONE is entitled to personal information shared in confidence to an elder or pastor. NO ONE.

Type Three Question: Satan's Device used for the purpose of self-exaltation through the fall of another.

Example: Mark 8:11 – And the Pharisees came forth, and began to question Him (Jesus), seeking of Him a sign from heaven, TEMPTING HIM.

Luke 11:54 – (The Pharisees) laying in wait for Him (Jesus), and seeking to catch something out of his mouth, THAT THEY MIGHT ACCUSE HIM.

Note: This is a popular tactic used by the media during an election year. The more debates, forums, interviews, etc… the greater the possibility of a gaffe that can be used against the candidate. With that tactic in mind, putting a brother or sister on display for debate is NOT of God!

Be sure of your faith in the Word of God and use it as the absolute standard. Man will waver, but God is unchanging.

Malachi 3:6 – For I am the Lord, I change not.

Revelation 1:8 – I am the Alpha and Omega, the beginning and the ending, saith the Lord, which is, and which was, and which is to come, the Almighty.

Checkup

Are you allowing Satan to use you against true brothers and sisters who love Christ and strive to live according to His word?

Notes:

_____

_____

_____

_____

_____

_____

_____

_____

Step 2: The Squeeze

Far too many homes today are allowing themselves to be squeezed into a world system that God never intended them to be a part of.

I John 2:15 – "Love not the world, neither the things that are in the world."

I John 2:16 – "For all that is in the world, the lust of the flesh, and the lust of the eyes, and the pride of life, is not of the Father, but is of the world."

Arguably, I believe financial pressure is tops on the list. Most families will take on far too much debt, putting both husband and wife into a vice of worldly pressure they were not intended by God to endure.

Proverbs 22:7 – "The rich ruleth over the poor, and the borrower is servant to the lender."

Luke 14:28 – "For which of you, intending to build a tower, sitteth not down first, and counteth the cost, whether he have sufficient to finish it?"

Due to mounting debt, schedules can no longer be optional or flexible, and connections with children and the marital relationships are often strained. But the lie takes root in the belief that the family must be a part of the secular system if they plan to 'succeed'. Weeks pass, then months, then years, with very little time spent nurturing the marriage or teaching the children. The family dinner has been replaced with practice schedules.

The family prayer-time no longer exists because loads of homework commandeer evening hours, stretching into the night. Instruction has been put in the hands of teachers, coaches, and friends. As the children grow, so does the pressure to compete with other families. (i.e. If the Jones' kid is playing sports then the pressure grows to be sure our little Johnny plays sports as well. If the Jones' kid graduates and gets a scholarship to a secular university, then ours will too!)

The squeeze is very evident in the marriage relationship as moms and dads pull in different directions with their individual careers and interests. Soon the marriage becomes more about the individual and less and less about becoming one flesh, striving together for God's purpose and order of the home.

With never a single thought as to what our sons and daughters will be taught and the tens of thousands spent to pay the high salaries of atheistic professors which ends in a diploma attached to an automatic hole of enormous debt, the cycle of financial bondage continues.

Prayer and seeking the will of God concerning our marriages and children is no longer considered an option. Why? The lie has been firmly planted in the minds of families that the world system is the ONLY path to success. Anything outside this box will end in sure disaster. This, my friend, is the SQUEEEEEEZE! And it introduces Step 3.

Checkup

Are you being squeeeeezed by Satan?

If so, how?

What changes need to be made to make your home more peaceful?

What can you do personally to bring about that peace?

Notes:

_____

_____

_____

_____

_____

Step 3: The Separation

We know that Adam and Eve walked with God through the garden in the cool of the day. They talked and fellowshipped with Him. I suppose you could say that Adam and Eve went to church together. But, Satan's next objective was to separate Eve from Adam by tempting her with something 'better'. Satan would successfully separate her from the companion who loved and walked with God consistently.

There are many ways in which Satan can separate and isolate. He can entice with the lust of the flesh and the pride of life. Another very effective method is found in Proverbs 16:28 where he uses his 'hissing' characteristic. "A froward man soweth strife: and a **whisperer** separateth chief friends." Ahhh, yes! This is what family feuds and church splits are made of!

In our culture, 'whispering' can come in many forms. It can be done through the physical act itself, or through texting, messaging, internet sites, and emails. The main objective is to separate and isolate from brothers and sisters who will influence in a godly direction. Many times people will turn from one another and six months down the road, can't even remember why. This is because a whisperer did their thinking for them, and without prayer or seeking God, they made life-changing decisions based on nothing more than the opinion of a whisperer who was continually in their ear.

The word 'froward' is defined as: unyielding, apt to complain, refractory (a person in constant opposition).

When a worldly and carnal mindset infiltrates the body of Christ, division is sure to follow if not dealt with. (Galatians 5:9)

Checkup

Have you allowed a 'whisperer' to bring strife between you and a fellow believer?

Is there a froward man/woman that you need to distance yourself from?

Notes:

_____

_____

_____

_____

_____

_____

_____

_____

_____

Step 4: <u>The Deception</u>

John 8:44 "…When he speaketh a lie, he speaketh of his own: for he is a liar, and the father of it."

Examples of Satan's Lies:

It's okay to look at that website. God created you with needs and desires, so He will understand and you can keep singing in the choir.

As a man, it's okay to talk to that woman who is unhappy at home. We should reach out to the hurting, right?

It's alright if you want to engage in open marriage. After all, it's better than divorce.

If you sow discord among the brethren, it's okay. They need to know how you feel and understand your viewpoint. Besides, it isn't really sowing discord. You're just sharing information.

That music is fun. You listened to it when you were a teen and it brings back a lot of good memories. Even if the lyrics promote sex, alcohol, and secular humanism, good memories can't be bad! Right?

Checkup

Do you have 'secret sins' that you think no one knows about?

Are you willing to do whatever it takes to remove that sin from your life?

Notes:

_____

_____

_____

_____

_____

_____

_____

_____

_____

Step 5 : The 'Gotcha'

This is where Satan is an absolute master. He can orchestrate a no-win situation for his target with complete precision. Every preceding step is to put his target in this position.

Adam was placed in a precarious position that demanded a decision – a decision that would alter the course of mankind. II Timothy 2:14 "Adam was not deceived, but the woman."

If Adam took and ate of the fruit, he would die. If Adam refused, he would live but the love of his heart would die. It was Satan's classic "Gotcha".

Satan enjoys trying to orchestrate situations where there is no winner and everyone is damaged. If he can bring down a pastor, it effects the entire congregation. If he brings down a husband or wife, son or daughter, it affects the entire household.

God's word tells us in I Corinthians 10:13 "God is faithful, who will not suffer you to be tempted above that ye are able; but will with the temptation also make a way to escape, that ye may be able to bear it."

The 'escape' that God provides may come in the form of turning away from tempting situations, or simply finding comfort in study and prayer that will help you endure the valley.

Checkup

Are you making judgments in situations before knowing all the facts?

Do you turn to God's word for comfort or do you look for an 'escape' in sports, amusement, or hobbies?

Notes:

_____

_____

_____

_____

_____

_____

_____

_____

_____

Step 6: Self-glory

Satan's fall came from a jealous desire to be worshipped and to steal all glory and honor from God. (Matthew 4:8, Isaiah 14:14)

Self-glory is anything but Christ-like. Phillippians 2:8 "And being found in fashion as a man, he humbled himself, and became obedient unto death, even the death of the cross."

Too often, we see Christian service and leadership glorified. Honor and respect for leaders are certainly in order. However, when church leadership is glamourized what message are we sending to the younger generation? Many times we see youth in love with what they believe is the lifestyle of a church leader, rather than cultivating a true servant's heart that will get down in the mud with everyone else, roll up their sleeves, and be the first man in and the last man out.

The mature Christian should encourage, but not push anyone into a responsibility they are clearly not ready to tackle. A call to lead, is a call to learn. It is never about 'self'. Discipline and a time-tested lifestyle of wisdom wrapped in humility is essential. If an individual is not willing to humble themselves at the feet of Jesus and learn, they are not fit to stand and minister in any capacity. Service and leadership must be preceded by a complete emptying of 'self'. The only 'self' needed is self-control.

Social media has taken mankind to a whole new level of self-glory. So, you helped your neighbor and posted pictures of yourself doing so. What if no one ever knew of your 'sacrifice' but you and God? Would you still do it? There's your heart test.

If your 'calling' or 'compassion' hinges on self-gratification, glory, pats on the back, a certain amount of money, or the assurance that everyone will know what a wonderful, caring person you are, don't expect reward in heaven. You are enjoying all the reward you will ever have right here.

Checkup

If no one ever said 'thank you' or patted you on the back, would you still serve?

Do you keep going in the face of obstacles?

Who do you serve? God or self?

Notes:

_____

_____

_____

_____

Step 7: The Blame Game

The final blow is very important since it restrains a man from confessing and repentance before God. When God asked Adam if he had sinned against his instruction he replied, "The woman whom thou gavest to be with me, she gave me of the tree, and I did eat." The woman had an excuse as well. "The serpent beguiled me, and I did eat."

Adam and Eve hid themselves from God (Genesis 3:7) by seeking justification of their actions through self-reliance and secular reasoning. Proverbs 3:7 "Be not wise in thine own eyes: fear the Lord and depart from evil."

Amnon sought guidance from a carnal friend, and it ultimately cost him his life. Saul sought wisdom of a Spirit guide/witch and it cost him his kingdom. Wisdom that is sought from any source other than that of Almighty God or godly council is vain.

James 1:5 "If any of you lack wisdom, let him ask of God, that giveth to all men liberally, and upbraideth not; and it shall be given him."

Checkup

Have you truly sought God and asked for His help, or do you rely on friends, family, and media to instruct your spirit?

Self-examination is sometimes a difficult, but necessary procedure!

Do you close God out of secret rooms in your heart?

How candid and blunt are you in your prayer life concerning your own sin and short-comings?

Notes:

_____

_____

_____

_____

_____

_____

_____

_____

_____

When Trials Come

Of course, we understand that Satan also had his way with Job but God called him 'perfect', and Job proved his love for God in the face of family and 'friends' criticism by his constant devotion and he sinned not. (Job 1:22)

Job did not fall prey to Satan as a result of walking the wrong path and falling for trickery out of ignorance. Sometimes trials come to bring us closer to our Lord, but proper biblical judgment will discern between a trial allowed of God to sharpen his servant, and one that is wrought as a result of a direct lack of study concerning the enemy's devices and the identification of sin.

In I John 4:1-5 we are admonished "believe not every spirit, but try the spirits whether they are of God: because many false prophets are gone out into the world. Hereby know ye the Spirit of God: Every spirit that confesseth that Jesus Christ is come in the flesh is of God: And every spirit that confesseth not that Jesus Christ is come in the flesh is not of God."

When we daily walk in the light of God's word, He will guide us into all truth. This doesn't guarantee that we won't have difficulties or that opposition won't arise. In fact, II Timothy 3:12 assures us, "Yea, and all that will live godly in Christ Jesus shall suffer persecution." Anyone who teaches otherwise is unbiblical.

However, trials can be self-inflicted if we are not walking according to God's commandments. This is why daily self-evaluation is absolutely necessary!

Notes:

_____

_____

_____

_____

_____

_____

_____

_____

_____

III – Fighting The Adversary

So, How Do We Fight The Good Fight?

Study, study, study!!!

II Timothy 2:15 "Study to shew thyself approved unto God, a workman that needeth not to be ashamed, rightly dividing the word of truth."

WARNING! Do your own studying and praying. Don't depend on someone else to do it for you, whether it be a family member, coworker, or (God forbid) social media or search engines. This is dangerous as you could be quite easily misled. If godly council is needed for a conflict, go to a party with no ulterior motive to the situation who is consistently godly and of mature years. (For example, it would be foolish to gain advice concerning a church matter from someone who has left the fellowship. An ungodly man would seize the opportunity to grind his axe.) Bitterness can also entice someone to advise amiss.

Checkup

Who or what do you rely on when troubles come?

When do you study?

Notes:

_____

_____

_____

_____

_____

_____

_____

_____

How To Know If You Are Being Counseled Wisely

James 3:13-18 – "Who is a wise man and endued with knowledge among you? Let him shew out of a good conversation his works with meekness of wisdom. But if ye have bitter envying and strife in your hearts, glory not, and lie not against the truth. This wisdom descendeth not from above, but is earthly, sensual, devilish. For where envying and strife is, there is confusion and every evil work. But the wisdom that is from above is first pure, then peaceable, gentle, and easy to be intreated, full of mercy and good fruits, without partiality, and without hypocrisy."

James is telling us that if we receive council that brings about bitterness, envying, and strife among true believers, this advice is not of God, but rather it is earthly, sensual, and devilish. This council will bring confusion and evil works. Ultimately, the bitterness, envying, and strife will have to be dealt with among the brethren causing hurt and disappointment to the entire body. This is in regard to all parties involved who are believers in Christ.

An unbeliever cannot be reasoned with on a spiritual level, as I Corinthians 2:14 teaches, "But the natural man receiveth not the things of the Spirit of God: for they are foolishness unto him: neither can he know them, because they are spiritually discerned." Therefore, if a party is of a carnal mind or entertains a secular worldview, division rather than compromise will be the outcome.

Checkup

Do you seek advice from consistent believers?

Do you seek God or use secular devices for answers?

Notes:

_____

_____

_____

_____

_____

_____

_____

_____

_____

Pray!

James 5:16 – "Confess your faults one to another, and pray one for another, that ye may be healed. The effectual fervent prayer of a righteous man availeth much."

I Thessalonians 5:17 tells us to "pray without ceasing." This does not imply that we walk through life with our eyes closed. On the contrary, we are to live with our eyes wide open as we talk to God throughout the day! When faced with a matter of uncertainty, we have the wonderful privilege of stopping to ask, "Lord, what should I do about this?" When enjoying a blessing, we have the opportunity to say, "Lord, I praise you!" When blessed with nourishment, we have the opportunity to say, "Lord, thank you for providing my food today."

Prayer for one another is critical. Your church leaders especially need your prayer, as they are under constant attack.

David had two pivotal people in his life; Jonathan and the prophet, Nathan. To be properly balanced, we need both. Jonathan was a helper, friend, and confidante. Nathan was not a constant nag or critic, but a necessary reminder of David's accountability to God. A believer with no Jonathan will become discouraged. A believer with no Nathan will become dangerous. Pray that God will not only give you a Jonathan and Nathan, but that you will recognize and appreciate the need for both.

Checkup

Does your lifestyle reflect your prayer life?

Do you set aside a time to pray?

Do you pray for the people in your church family?

Do you pray for your church leaders more than you criticize or give of your opinion?

Notes:

_____

_____

_____

_____

_____

_____

_____

_____

_____

Self-Control!

James 3:5,6 – "Even so the tongue is a little member, and boasteth great things. Behold, how great a matter a little fire kindleth! And the tongue is a fire, a world of iniquity: so is the tongue among our members, that it defileth the whole body, and setteth on fire the course of nature; and it is set on fire of hell."

Proverbs 25:28 – "He that hath no rule over his own spirit is like a city that is broken down, and without walls."

Romans 12:1,2 – "I beseech you therefore brethren by the mercies of God, that ye present your bodies a living sacrifice, holy, acceptable unto God, which is your reasonable service. And be not conformed to this world but be ye transformed by the renewing of your mind that ye may prove what is that good, and acceptable, and perfect will of God."

Proverbs 16:32 – "He that is slow to anger is better than the mighty; and he that ruleth his spirit than he that taketh a city."

Galatians 5:23 – "Meekness, temperance: against such there is no law."

James 1:20 – "For the wrath of man worketh not the righteousness of God."

Proverbs 15:1 – "A soft answer turneth away wrath."

WARNING! <u>Never</u> approach a brother or sister in anger. Condition of the heart and tone of voice can make or break your effectiveness in attempting to resolve a conflict. Pardon the oxymoron, but a soft answer speaks volumes!

Checkup

Do you exhibit immaturity in your character such as emotional outbursts or pouting?

Do you provoke fellow believers by your accusations or tantrums?

Notes:

_____

_____

_____

_____

_____

_____

_____

Beware!

Romans 16:17,18 "Mark them which cause divisions … and avoid them!"

Be wary of a double-minded man (or woman). This is an individual who changes their position based on friendships, popular demand, or what is personally expedient. James 1:8 – "A double- minded man is unstable in all his ways." So, choose your words carefully with someone who cannot be trusted to consistently uphold truth.

Proverbs 4:24-26 "Put away from thee a froward mouth." (Note: Whether it's your mouth or someone else's - get rid of it.)

Galatians 6:10 – "As we have therefore opportunity, let us do good unto all men, ESPECIALLY unto them who are of the household of faith."

If we are unkind to our brothers and sisters in Christ, how can we say we are full of love and compassion?

Checkup

Do you spend time with people who are inconsistent in their walk with Christ?

Is there someone who constantly approaches you with criticism of others?

Notes:

_____

_____

_____

_____

_____

_____

_____

_____

_____

Walk Humbly and Consistantly

Romans 12:10 – "Be kindly affectioned one to another with brotherly love; in honour preferring one another."

Was someone else asked to teach a Bible Class? Did another sing the solo? Remember, David was asked to simply keep the sheep – a job that was by no means glamorous. But, he performed his duty consistently and joyfully. David proved over time that he could be trusted, and the little shepherd boy became king. You may never be well-known, but great is the reward of those who are faithful. It's all about the glory of God – not the glory of man.

Checkup

Do you display a heart of contentment with what God has given you to do?

Are you secretly jealous of others?

Notes:

_____

_____

_____

_____

Do YOUR Job!

Refrain from policing everyone else and do your own job. What have YOU been given to do? If you have been given a responsibility, then do it and you won't have time to whisper about how someone else is performing their task.

I Thessalonians 4:11 "Study to be quiet, and do YOUR OWN BUSINESS, and work with your own hands."

Proverbs 20:3 – "It is an honour for a man to cease from strife: but every fool will be meddling."

Proverbs 24:2 – "For their heart studieth destruction, and their lips talk of mischief."

II Thessalonians 3:11 – "For we hear that there are some which walk among you disorderly, working not at all, but are busybodies." (Gossiping is a stereotype of women, but don't fool yourself. Men are pros.)

Checkup

Do you complain about others while failing to attend
your own place of service?

Are you so busy meddling into someone else's job in the
church, that you fail to put the energy needed into your
own?

Notes:

_____

_____

_____

_____

_____

_____

_____

_____

Keep and Teach!

We often hear the cliché, "The church is only as strong as the homes that make it up." Understand the importance of keeping the home safe and peaceful, and the role of teaching godly lifestyle as pleasing unto God.

Women are to follow instruction from Titus 2:3-5 – "... be in behavior as becometh holiness, not false accusers, not given to much wine, teachers of good things; that they may teach the young women to be sober, to love their husbands, to love their children, to be discreet, chaste, keepers at home, good, obedient to their own husbands, that the word of God be not blasphemed."

Men are instructed to teach the young men to be, "Sober-minded. In all things shewing thyself a pattern of good works: in doctrine shewing uncorruptness, gravity, sincerety, sound speech, that cannot be condemned" Titus 2:6-8

When Nehemiah was compelled by God to set watchmen on the wall, he also set each man over his own family with swords, spears, and bows. When it comes to your family, have the grit to fight for its spiritual welfare!

Checkup

Is Christ honored in your home? If not, what needs to change?

How can you be instrumental in making that change?

If Christ rode in your car, would you quickly change the radio station?

Does your family entertainment include movies with profanity and premarital promiscuity?

Is the Holy Spirit welcome or grieved in your home?

Notes:

_____

_____

_____

_____

_____

_____

_____

_____

Handle A Conflict Discretely And Keep It Confidential!

Matthew 18:15 "If thy brother shall trespass against thee, go and tell him his fault between thee and him alone: if he shall hear thee, thou hast gained thy brother. But if he will not hear thee, then take with thee one or two more, that in the mouth of two or three witnesses every word may be established."

NEVER! Trust Your Emotions ...

Jeremiah 17:9 "The heart is deceitful above all things, and desperately wicked: who can know it?"

TRUST God's Word

Psalm 119:105 "Thy word is a lamp unto my feet, and a light unto my path."

Checkup

Do you repeat confidential matters via tongue, phone, or keyboard?

Notes:

_____

_____

_____

_____

_____

_____

_____

_____

_____

Protect Your Testimony At All Costs!

Staying close to the Lord will help in a time of temptation. Don't be fooled. Temptation can come inside the church walls as well as without. If an individual tempts you with provocative dress, flirtatious conversation, or tempts you to anger, avoid them. Show kindness when they are in your path, but never place yourself in a situation that would entice you to sin. Do you remember Joseph's action when Potipher's wife attempted to seduce him? He FLED!

Proverbs 22:1- "A good name is rather to be chosen than great riches."

Checkup

What is your testimony among fellow students, customers, or co-workers?

Notes:

_____

_____

_____

_____

Avoid Laziness

We hear much about homosexuality and assume it was the only sin of Sodom, but Ezekiel 16:49 describes it much differently. "Behold, this was the iniquity of thy sister Sodom; pride, fullness of bread, and abundance of idleness was in her and in her daughters, neither did she strengthen the hand of the poor and needy."

Sexual perversion was never mentioned. It was pride, gluttony, and laziness. These were the sins that ultimately led to sexual perversion. A man with too much idle time is dangerous.

II Thessalonians 3:11 – "For we hear that there are some which walk among you disorderly, working not at all, but are busybodies."

Eccelesiastes 9:10 "Whatsoever thy hand findeth to do, do it with thy might;"

Stay busy about your responsibilities and refrain from idleness if you want to stay out of trouble. In short, mind your own business and get to work!

Checkup

How much idle time do you have per day?

How can you fill you idle time with productively that honors God?

Do you consistently criticize the workings of the church, but fail to show up for work days or activities?

Notes:

_____

_____

_____

_____

_____

_____

_____

_____

_____

_____

_____

Don't Become Anemic

II Timothy 3:16-17 – "All scripture is given by inspiration of God, and is profitable for doctrine, for reproof, for correction, for instruction in righteousness:

Psalm 119:11 - "Thy word have I hid in mine heart, that I might not sin against thee."

Proverbs 3:1,2 – "My son, forget not my law; but let thine heart keep my commandments."

Show me a Christian who relies solely on their Pastor or Sunday School teacher for spiritual nourishment, and I'll show you a weak and immature Christian. Help from the Lord through the week can be accomplished in many ways! Read your bible. If you're on the road, listen to the word of God on CD or radio! Listen to Christ-honoring music. Get in the habit of talking to your heavenly Father about everything!

Just as the physical body needs daily food, so does the soul. Remember the old adage: *An army travels on its stomach.* Lack of nourishment yields a very weak, easy-to-beat soldier.

Checkup

Do you have Christ-honoring music in your vehicle?

Do you enjoy strong Bible preaching and teaching?

Notes:

_____

_____

_____

_____

_____

_____

_____

_____

_____

Get Rid Of The Junk Food!

Romans 6:1-2 – "What shall we say then? Shall we continue in sin, that grace may abound? God forbid. How shall we, that are dead to sin, live any longer therein?"

If we are not willing to deal with the sin in our lives, how dare we expect a holy God to bless our efforts!

Galatians 6:7 – "Be not deceived; God is not mocked: for whatsoever a man soweth, that shall he also reap."

Checkup

What needs to go from your life in order to have pure fellowship with God?

Notes:

_____

_____

_____

_____

Throw Away The Binoculars And Use A Mirror On A Daily Basis.

Psalm 139:23,24 "Search me, O God, and know my heart: try me, and know my thoughts: and see if there be any wicked way in ME, and lead me in the way of everlasting."

Matthew 7:3-5 "And why beholdest thou the mote that is in thy brother's eye, but considerest not the beam that is in thine own eye?"

Regular self-evaluation will go a looooooong way in keeping the proper perspective of self and others, and most importantly, God.

Checkup

How often do you thoroughly examine your own life?

Notes:

_____

_____

_____

_____

_____

_____

Commitment!!!

Here is where we bog down. 'Commitment' is probably the most unsettling word in American culture. We have become a society that is no longer committed to our marriages, our children, our employer, our local church of believers, and the list goes on and on.

It has become too easy to be involved, yet uncommitted. Our laws and culture have made it increasingly convenient and even rewarding to simply live together instead of commit to each other in holy matrimony. It's easier to let the coaches, teachers, and baby sitters bear the responsibility of child training. It's easier to complain about the employer, than be committed to the job and earn the raise or promotion. Finally, it's easier to simply meld into a congregation and enjoy all the benefits received from the work and commitment of others, while refusing to commit yourself – just in case something happens that you don't agree with or you simply decide that the church down the road is more exciting for your kids.

It is grossly selfish and disrespectful to fellow brothers and sisters in Christ who labor in the ministry, when people view them as completely optional. (i.e. If nothing else is going on, I might attend the men's fellowship or help with the Christmas presentation. But I won't commit, in case something else pops up that I would rather do that night).

There was a time in America when parents told the coach, "My child will not be able to practice or play on

Sunday. That's the Lord's day and we go to church for worship." Those are the bygone days. Believers without a firm biblical worldview, will commit themselves to the secular without even realizing it.

II Timothy 3:1-5 This know also, that in the last days perilous times shall come. For men shall be lovers of their own selves ... lovers of pleasures more than lovers of God.

Have you considered the time your pastor took to pray and present a message? What about the Sunday School teacher? How about the lady who cooked all day for the ladies meeting? Or the men who spent their Saturday constructing props for the Christmas presentation? Or the Youth Director who gave his day to plan an outreach? Does this mean something to you? Or is it purely optional whether or not you attend?

I'm not implying that everyone quit their job and live in the church basement. Nor am I referring to the unavoidable events in life. Let's face it – sickness and emergencies happen. I'm also completely aware of church leaders who abuse their authority by asking and expecting the UNreasonable. However, most pastors and church leaders are in an ongoing battle with discouragement due to the lack of concern and interest. Can you imagine a local ministry where everyone gave what was reasonable? A fellowship of believers where everyone pulls their own weight instead of waiting for (and expecting) someone else to do it? A congregation with a mind to work would be a breath of fresh air to anyone who's been carrying the load.

From the pulpit to the back door, we must ask ourselves why we chose to become a part of the group of believers to which we belong. Was is to worship God in spirit and truth as we try to be a blessing to our fellow brothers and sisters in Christ? Or did we come with a what-can-you-do-for-me mindset? Did we come to empty our pockets or hope to pad our pockets? Did we come with a love for the people or are we looking for people to serve US? Motive will certainly dictate commitment and 'stick-ability'. A true love for the brethren would surely put a stop to the revolving door in churches today – from the front to the back.

I'm afraid we all suffer from a severe case of UNthankfulness and lack of appreciation. Fellow believers who live in countries where they must meet in secret or be put to death for their faith, would undoubtedly shake their heads in sorrow at the complete lack of concern and hunger for the gospel in America.

People died for the Bible you hold in your hand. People died for your freedom to worship. People died today in a foreign country because they chose to worship in the face of persecution. The holy, Lamb of God died so you wouldn't have to face the wrath of Almighty God in hell for eternity … or does any of that even matter anymore?

2 Timothy 3:1-5 This know also, that in the last days perilous times shall come. For men shall be lovers of their own selves, covetous, boasters, proud, blasphemers, disobedient to parents, UNTHANKFUL, unholy.

Checkup:

If your children were asked which was more important to your family, church or school activities, what would their answer be?

Do you tell the coach that your child won't play or practice on Sunday, or does the coach dictate to your family when you will or will not attend worship?

If everyone in the congregation had the same level of commitment as you, would there be a church where families could hear the gospel?

When asked to participate or help, do you give of yourself with joy or make excuses why you cannot help and then criticize how it was done?

Are you looking to help or be helped?

Notes:

_____

_____

_____

_____

_____

_____

ENCOURAGE!!!

I Thessalonians 5:11 – "Wherefore comfort yourselves together, and edify one another, even as also ye do."

Colossians 3:16 – "Let the word of Christ dwell in you richly in all wisdom; teaching and admonishing one another in psalms and hymns and spiritual songs, singing with grace in your hearts to the Lord."

Send a card! Give a call! Cook a meal! Make a visit! Nothing gets our eyes off of **self** quite like being an encouragement to someone else.

Checkup

Do you try to be kind to others or is it all about you?

Are you snobbish in feeling you haven't received the attention you feel you so richly deserve?

Notes:

_____

_____

_____

_____

_____

_____

Consideration

Romans 12:10 – Be kindly affectioned one to another with brotherly love; in honour preferring one another.

Do not demand of others what you are unwilling to do yourself.

Example: Help the laborers by making them as comfortable as possible. If it's hot, try to keep them cool with a fan or refreshments. If it's cold, offer a blanket and coffee. If you are having an event that will entail long hours, offer a meal. Do as much as possible to accommodate the situation if you plan to ask for participation down the road. Otherwise, plan to do it yourself when no one shows.

Consider the following story of the Revolutionary War:

A rider on horseback came across a squad of soldiers who were trying to move a heavy piece of timber.

A corporal stood by, shouting superior orders to "Heave!"

But the piece of timber was too heavy for the squad.

"Why don't you help them?" asked the quiet man on the horse, addressing the haughty corporal.

"Me? Why, I'm a corporal sir!"

Dismounting, the stranger carefully took his place with the soldiers.

"Now, all together boys – heave!" he said. And the big piece of timber slid into place.

The stranger mounted his horse and addressed the corporal as he revealed his uniform. "The next time you have a piece of timber for your men to handle, corporal, send for your commander-in-chief."

The stunned corporal looked at the horseman - George Washington, the first American President.

Leadership is an attitude of servitude toward your people.

And respect isn't earned by staying on your high horse, but from getting down, rolling up your sleeves, and getting your hands dirty.

I Peter 1:9 – Use hospitality one to another.

If the laymen see their leaders going over and beyond, they will go the extra mile, as well. However, if the laymen feel they are being used, while the leader sits on his high horse, there will soon be an attitude of discouragement, followed by division. If you want to win hands, you must first win hearts.

Ask Forgiveness

You were expecting the heading to say, Be Forgiving. Right? While having a forgiving heart is a wonderful thing, I'm afraid our culture has teetered the scales until all the weight has landed solely on the shoulders of the abused, while the abuser sits in pious innocence, holding up their "Don't Judge Me" sign. We have taught forgiveness in such a lop-sided manner that it has produced a generation of arrogance with a you-owe-me attitude. The thought process goes something like this; "I know I was out of line when I told off my sister, but the Bible says she is supposed to forgive me, so I don't owe her an apology." Thus we have scores of people sitting on church pews secure in the knowledge that no matter what offense they commit, they are covered by the let's-all-be-forgiving clause. My friend, nothing could be further from the truth. We have a responsibility to God and man to humbly and sincerely ask forgiveness of those we have abused and disrespected. (Matthew 5:23, 24) (James 5:16) (Luke 17: 1-4)

Checkup

Am I completely innocent of any and all wrongdoing or disrespect toward my brothers and sisters in Christ?

Do I have unhindered fellowship with God and man?

IV – Addressing The Adversary's Battleground

Administer Discipline As A Last Resort!

Galatians 6:1 – Brethren, if a man be overtaken in a fault, ye which are spiritual, **restore** such an one in the spirit of meekness; considering thyself, lest thou also be tempted.

Attempt to lovingly lead a fallen brother/sister back to Christ. But if all attempts fail …

I Corinthians 5:11 – But now I have written unto you **not to keep company**, if any man that is called a brother be a fornicator, or covetous, or an idolater, or a railer, or a drunkard, or an extortioner; with such an one no not to eat.

Fornicator – An unmarried person, male or female, who has criminal conversation with the other sex; also a married man who has sexual commerce with an unmarried woman.

Covetous – Very desirous. Eager to obtain.

Idolater – One who pays divine honors to images,

statues, or representations of anything made by hands; one who worships as a deity that which is not God.

Railer – One who scoffs, insults, censures or reproaches with words.

Drunkard – A person who is habitually or frequently drunk.

Extortioner – To draw away from by force. Undue exercise of power.

Titus 3:10 – A man that is an heretick after the first and second admonition **reject**.

Heretic – Anyone who maintains erroneous opinions.

II Thessalonians 3:6 – Now we command you, brethren, in the name of our Lord Jesus Christ, that ye **withdraw yourselves** from every brother that walketh disorderly, and not after the tradition which he received of us.

Romans 16:17-18 – Now I beseech you, brethren, **mark them** which cause divisions and offences contrary to the doctrine which ye have learned; and **avoid them**.

II Timothy 2:16-18 – But **shun** profane and vain babblings: for they will increase unto more ungodliness.

Note: These admonitions are all inclusive meaning any individual whether they be layman or leader.

V – Weaknesses of The Adversary

Satan isn't an omniscient, omnipresent, or omnipotent diety. Unlike God Almighty, he is a created being with limitations. Therefore, he can be battled with the help of our Lord.

Ephesians 6:11 instructs us to "put on the whole armour of God, that ye may be able to stand against the wiles of the devil."

James 4:7 says we must "submit … therefore to God. Resist the devil, and he will flee."

Satan only knows what we allow him to know. Be aware each time you speak - he is listening. If there is a weakness, ask the Lord for help in silence. Don't give your enemy ammunition by telling him your weak points!

In Matthew 4, Satan tempts Christ and Christ fires back with the Word Of God! If we study and know what God said in His word, we will be more apt to identify a lie or temptation.

And finally, always remember …

Ephesians 6:12 "For we wrestle not against flesh and blood, but against principalities, against powers, against rulers of the darkness of this world, against spiritual wickedness in high places"

Notes:

_____

_____

_____

_____

_____

_____

Made in the USA
Columbia, SC
30 October 2022